To Ethan and Amelia and to all of Sophany's dancers—may this generation of children grow up together with hope for a brilliant future. —D.R.

For my dancer daughter, Kate, and her dancer friends Isabel, Apoorva, and Bella—C.H.

Khmer Translation

On pages 30-31 of this book is a translation of this story into the language of Cambodia, called Khmer (pronounced Ke-MY and, in some parts of the world, Ke-MARE), written in the traditional Indian script that originated thousands of years ago.

The creation of art for this book and the teaching of local Khmer dance are generously supported by Gardner Family Care Corporation.

g

GARDNER

The Cambodian Dancer

SOPHANY'S GIFT OF HOPE

by DARYN REICHERTER

illustrated by CHRISTY HALE

Khmer translation by BOPHAL PHEN

TUTTLE Publishing

Tokyo | Rutland, Vermont | Singapore

Sophany was a dancer in Cambodia.
She learned the ancient ways of dancing handed
down from generation to generation.

2

She learned how to
move her hands

and arms.

She learned how to look like the stone reliefs on the walls of the temples.

5

The dance gave her energy.

When Sophany grew up, she taught the dance to little girls.

8

She taught them how to move their hands.

She taught them
where to put their feet.

She even taught them
how to tilt their heads.

11

The dance gave the little girls energy too.

Sophany was one of the best dancers. She danced for huge crowds of people. She even danced before the King of Cambodia!

But then something terrible happened. Bad men took over the land. They were called the Khmer Rouge. They destroyed the land its people. They took away Sophany's dance and even destroyed the reliefs on the walls of the temples.

Many of the dancers disappeared. Those who were left
behind became as shadow puppets, secret and saddened.

The happiness of the dance was taken from them.
The energy of the dance was gone.

Lost and alone, Sophany was left with nothing but her shadow.
The Khmer Rouge had turned Cambodia into a shadow land.
Sophany was forced to move far away.

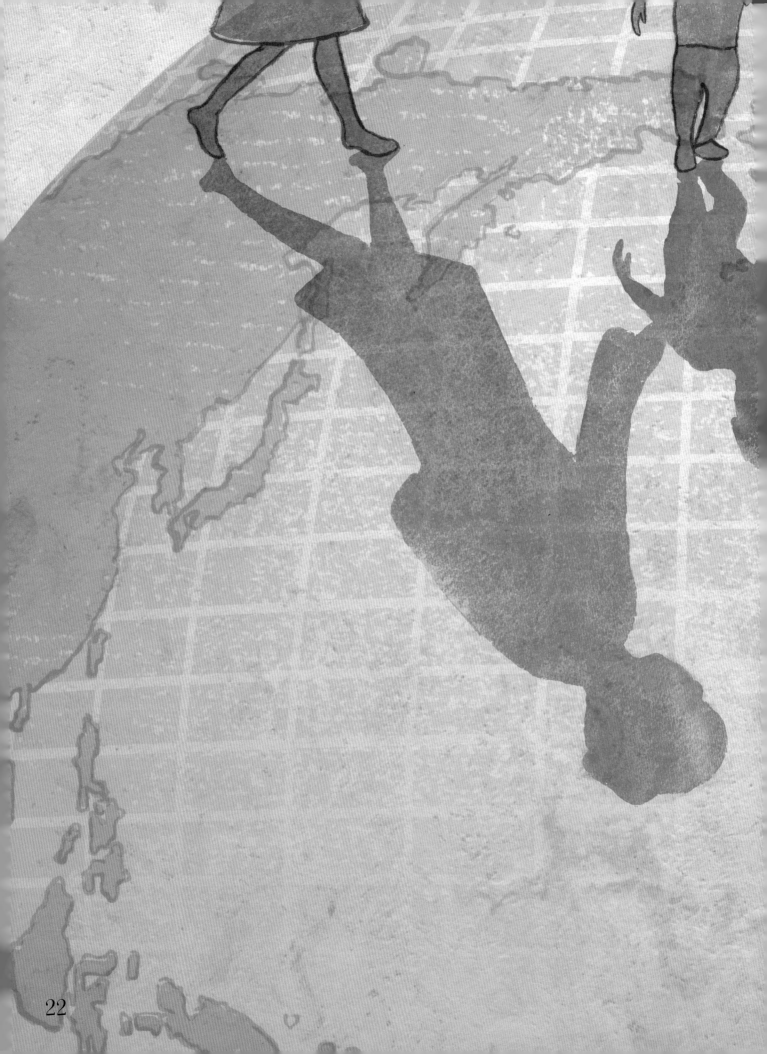

Many years later, on the other side of the world,
Sophany tried to help heal the wounds left by the
Khmer Rouge. Even though she had escaped to a free
land, she felt as if she were still a shadow.

When she saw that the Cambodian children growing up in
America did not know the dance of her lost home, she was sad.
It was as if the children were growing up as shadows too.

23

So she remembered the dance that was forced into hiding. She remembered how to move her hands and arms. She remembered how to look like the stone reliefs on the walls of the temples.

Dancing again made her feel happy and strong. The energy of the dance shone light onto the shadows.

Sophany created a school to teach the dance to the next generation of Cambodian girls.

She taught them how to move their hands.

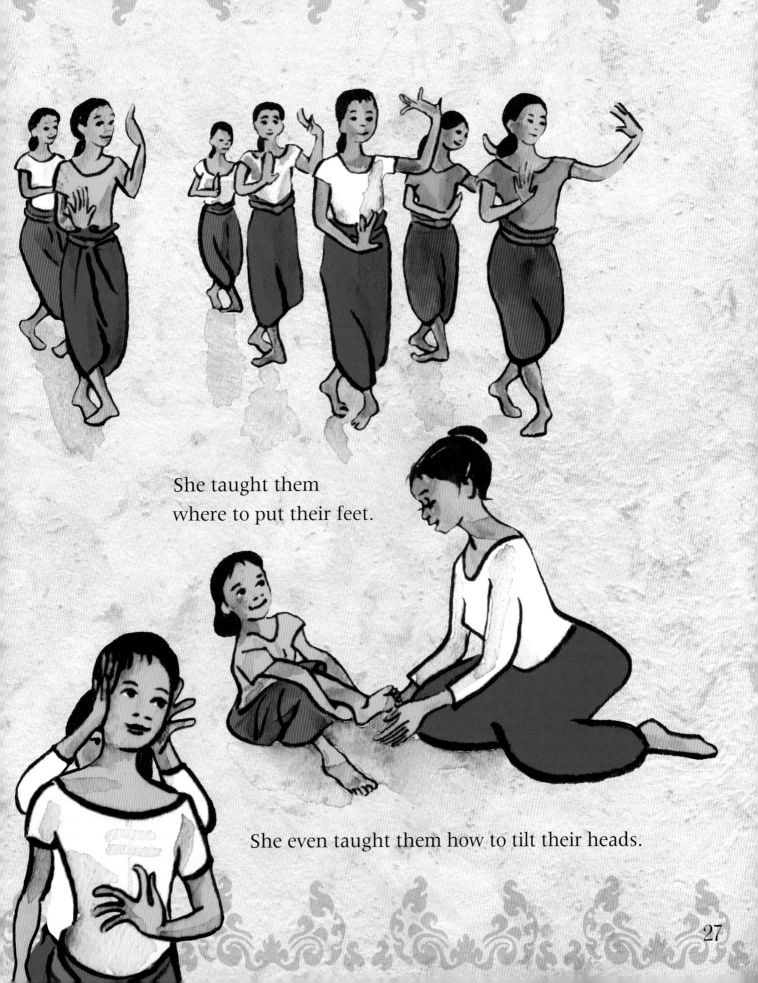

She taught them
where to put their feet.

She even taught them how to tilt their heads.

The dance gave the girls energy. The dance gave Sophany energy too.

Watching the girls, Sophany smiled. Now the shadows are gone.
Now there is dance again.

វិធីដែលសុផានីរក្សាការរាំរបាំ

(How Sophany Saved the Dance)

សុផានីធ្លាប់ជាអ្នករាំរបាំម្នាក់នៅក្នុងស្រុកខ្មែរ។

គាត់បានរៀនវិធីរាំរបាំបុរាណដែលបានបន្តគ្នាពីមួយជំនាន់ទៅមួយជំនាន់រាប់សតវត្សរ៍មកហើយ។

គាត់បានរៀនពីរបៀបពត់បត់បែនប្រអប់ដៃនិងដៃ។

គាត់បានរៀនវិធីធ្វើយ៉ាងណាឲ្យដូចរូបចម្លាក់ថ្មនៅតាមជញ្ជាំងនៃប្រាសាទនានា។

ការរាំរបាំបានធ្វើឲ្យគាត់មានកម្លាំង។

ពេលគាត់ធំឡើង, គាត់បានបង្រៀនការរាំរបាំទៅកុមារីតូចៗ។

គាត់បង្រៀនពួកគេពីរបៀបពត់បត់បែនដៃ។

គាត់បង្រៀនពួកគេពីកន្លែងដាក់ជើង។

គាត់ក៏បង្រៀនពួកគេពីរបៀបផ្អៀងក្បាលទៀតផង។

ការរាំរបាំធ្វើឲ្យពួកកុមារីតូចៗមានកម្លាំងដែរ។

សុផានីជាអ្នករាំរបាំម្នាក់ក្នុងបណ្តាអ្នករាំដ៏ល្អបំផុត។

គាត់បានរាំរបាំសម្រាប់ហ្វូងមនុស្សដ៏ធំៗ។

គាត់បានរាំនៅចំពោះមុខព្រះមហាក្សត្រខ្មែរទៀតផង។

ស្រាប់តែមានរឿងដ៏រន្ធត់បានកើតឡើង។

ពួកមនុស្សអាក្រក់បានគ្រប់គ្រងទឹកដី។

ពួកគេមានឈ្មោះថាជាខ្មែរក្រហម។

ពួកគេបានបំផ្លាញទឹកដីនិងប្រជាជន។

ពួកគេបានដកយកការរាំរបាំរបស់សុផានី ហើយបានបំផ្លាញអ្នករាំស្ទើរតែទាំងអស់។

ពួកគេថែមទាំងបំផ្លាញរូបចម្លាក់នៅតាមជញ្ជាំងប្រាសាទនានាទៀតផង។

អ្នករាំរបាំដែលនៅសេសសល់បានក្លាយទៅជាអាយ៉ងស្រមោល, អាថ៌កំបាំងនិងទុក្ខសោក។

សេចក្តីសុខដែលបានមកពីការរាំរបាំត្រូវគេដកហូតយកទៅបាត់។

កម្លាំងដែលបានមកពីការរាំរបាំក៏បាត់សាបសូន្យ។

វង្វេងហើយឯកា. សូផានីគ្មានសល់អ្វីសោះឡើយក្រៅពីស្រមោលរបស់គាត់។

ពួកខ្មែរក្រហមបានធ្វើឲ្យស្រុកខ្មែរក្លាយទៅជាទឹកដីស្រមោល។

សូផានីត្រូវគេបង្ខិតបង្ខំឲ្យចាកចេញទៅកាន់ទិវាឆ្ងាយ។

ច្រើនឆ្នាំក្រោយមក. នៅឯម្ដាងទៀតនៃពិភពលោក សូផានីព្យាយាមថែរក្សារូបស
ដែលពួកមនុស្សអាក្រក់បានបង្កឡើង។

ទោះបីជាគាត់បានភៀសខ្លួនរួចផុតពីពួកខ្មែរក្រហមក៏ដោយ. គាត់នៅតែមានអារម្មណ៍
ថាគាត់ជាស្រមោលងដែល។

ពេលគាត់សង្កេតឃើញកូនខ្មែរដែលធំធាត់នៅអាមេរិកមិនបានដឹងពីការរាំបាំ
របស់ស្រុកគាត់ដែលបានបាត់បង់ទៅ. គាត់ក៏កើតទុក្ខព្រួយ។

វាហាក់បីដូចជាកូនក្មេងទាំងនោះបានធំឡើងដូចជាស្រមោលអញ្ចឹងដែរ។

ដូច្នេះហើយ. គាត់ក៏រំលឹកឡើងវិញនូវការរាំបាំដែលត្រូវគេបង្ខំឲ្យលាក់ទុក។

គាត់រំលឹកឡើងវិញពីរបៀបរិធីគាត់បត់បែនដៃ។

គាត់រំលឹកឡើងវិញពីរបៀបធ្វើឲ្យដួចរូបចម្លាក់ថ្មដែលបិតនៅតាមជញ្ជាំងប្រាសាទនានា។

ការរាំបាំម្ដងទៀតបានធ្វើឲ្យគាត់មានអារម្មណ៍សប្បាយនិងខ្លាំងក្លាឡើងវិញ។

កម្លាំងនៃការរាំបាំបានជះពន្លឺទៅលើស្រមោលផ្សេងៗ។

សូផានីបានបង្កើតសាលារៀនដើម្បីបង្រៀនការរាំបាំដល់កូនក្មេងខ្មែរជំនាន់ក្រោយ។

គាត់បានបង្រៀនពួកគេពីរបៀបបត់បត់បែនដៃ។

គាត់បានបង្រៀនពួកគេពីកន្លែងដាក់ជើង។

គាត់ថែមទាំងបង្រៀនពួកគេពីរបៀបផ្ទៀងក្បាលទៀតផង។

ការរាំបាំបានធ្វើឲ្យពួកកុមារីមានកម្លាំង។

ការរាំបាំបានធ្វើឲ្យសូផានីមានកម្លាំងដែរ។

ពេលកំពុងមើលពួកកុមារី. សូផានីបានញញឹម។

ពន្លឺស្រមោលក៏បាត់សូន្យអស់។

ពន្លឺមានតែការរាំបាំម្ដងទៀតប៉ុណ្ណោះ។

AUTHOR'S NOTE: A TRUE STORY OF SURVIVAL

The Cambodian Dancer: Sophany's Gift of Hope was inspired by a true story. Sophany Bay really was a dancer in Cambodia. She was one of the best, often performing for huge crowds, even for royalty, just as it says in the story. When she grew up, she taught the dance to little girls.

But then a terrible thing happened. A group of men called the Khmer Rouge pushed their way into power. They abolished arts, culture, education and religion. They destroyed the land and its people. Cambodia became a place of great sorrow and fear.

Sophany lost her family at the hands of the Khmer Rouge. Though she was filled with grief she used her courage and her wits to escape from Cambodia to Thailand. After years in a Thai refugee camp, she was accepted as a refugee to the United States of America.

Sophany moved to San Jose, California. She learned English and went to college to study social work. After college she began working as a counselor for Cambodian survivors in America. She became a community leader and an advocate for human rights. She became one of the very few Cambodian American witnesses to testify in 2013 against the Khmer Rouge leaders. Her story helped to convict the leaders of their terrible crimes against the Cambodian people.

In her new life in the United States, Sophany looked for ways to help heal the Cambodian community. She saw that Cambodian children growing up in America did not know the culture of the homeland they had lost. It seemed to her that, even in this new safe land, Cambodian children were growing up in the shadows.

So she remembered the dance that had been forced into hiding. She remembered the joy and energy it had given her. Now, more than ever, she felt that it was important to share the dance with others. She created a program for teaching Khmer dance to children in San Jose. Dancing, and teaching the dance to others, made Sophany come alive again. Learning the dance has helped many children in the Cambodian community step out of the shadows.

Decades later, Sophany is still teaching the dance, and still working with Cambodian families to make their lives better.

She is the most resilient person I have ever known, or ever will know.

Thank you, Sophany!

The Tuttle Story:
"Books to Span the East and West"

Many people are surprised to learn that the world's leading publisher of books on Asia had humble beginnings in the tiny American state of Vermont. The company's founder, Charles E. Tuttle, belonged to a New England family steeped in publishing.

Immediately after WWII, Tuttle served in Tokyo under General Douglas MacArthur and was tasked with reviving the Japanese publishing industry. He later founded the Charles E. Tuttle Publishing Company, which thrives today as one of the world's leading independent publishers.

Though a westerner, Tuttle was hugely instrumental in bringing a knowledge of Japan and Asia to a world hungry for information about the East. By the time of his death in 1993, Tuttle had published over 6,000 books on Asian culture, history and art—a legacy honored by the Japanese emperor with the "Order of the Sacred Treasure," the highest tribute Japan can bestow upon a non-Japanese.

With a backlist of 1,500 titles, Tuttle Publishing is more active today than at any time in its past—still inspired by Charles Tuttle's core mission to publish fine books to span the East and West and provide a greater understanding of each.

Published by Tuttle Publishing, an imprint of Periplus Editions (HK) Ltd.

www.tuttlepublishing.com

Copyright © 2015 by Daryn Reicherter
Illustrations copyright © 2015 by Christy Hale

Library of Congress Control Number: 2015940443

ISBN 978-0-8048-4516-8

Distributed by

North America, Latin America & Europe
Tuttle Publishing
364 Innovation Drive
North Clarendon, VT 05759-9436 U.S.A.
Tel: (802) 773-8930
Fax: (802) 773-6993
info@tuttlepublishing.com
www.tuttlepublishing.com

Japan
Tuttle Publishing
Yaekari Building, 3rd Floor
5-4-12 Osaki, Shinagawa-ku
Tokyo 141 0032
Tel: (81) 3 5437-0171
Fax: (81) 3 5437-0755
sales@tuttle.co.jp
www.tuttle.co.jp

Asia Pacific
Berkeley Books Pte. Ltd.
61 Tai Seng Avenue #02-12
Singapore 534167
Tel: (65) 6280-1330
Fax: (65) 6280-6290
inquiries@periplus.com.sg
www.periplus.com

First edition
18 17 16 15   6 5 4 3 2 1   1507TWP

Printed in Malaysia

TUTTLE PUBLISHING® is a registered trademark of Tuttle Publishing, a division of Periplus Editions (HK) Ltd.